W9-AKE-244

Making a Book
by Althea
illustrated by Tim Hunkin

© 1981 Rourke Enterprises, Inc.
© 1980 Althea Braithwaite
© 1980 Tim Hunkin, Illustrations

Published by Rourke Enterprises, Inc., P.O. Box 929, Windermere, Florida 32786. Copyright © 1981 by Rourke Enterprises, Inc. All copyrights reserved. No part of this book may be reproduced in any form without written permission from the publisher. Printed in the United States of America.

Library of Congress Cataloging in Publication Data

Althea.
  Making a book.

  Summary: Describes the processes involved in making a book, from typesetting to binding.
    1. Printing, Practical—Juvenile literature.
  2. Books—Juvenile literature. I. Hunkin, Tim, ill.
  II. Title.
  Z244.A518 1981   686.2   81-13769
  ISBN 0-86592-567-4   AACR2

Rourke Enterprises, Inc.
Windermere, Florida 32786

The words for the book are typed
on a keyboard like a typewriter.
The words are stored on a computer
disk which looks like a record.
A long book will fit on one disk.
The words can then be printed
on paper for checking.

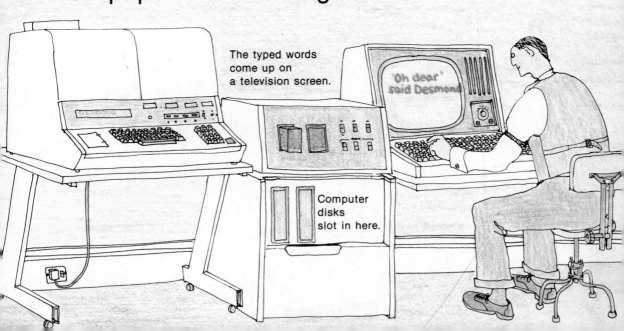

The typed words
come up on
a television screen.

'Oh dear'
said Desmond

Computer
disks
slot in here.

Words can be set with different size letters: small, medium, or large ones.

The very large words for the cover are set by hand, one letter at a time. Then they are printed on a piece of paper for checking.

The designer gathers the pieces of paper with the words and adds artwork for the pictures. She pastes both down on a stiff sheet of paper. The paper is the same size as the pages of the book.

All the pages are pasted on two very large sheets. This is called the final artwork.

Some of the pages are upside down. This is because after they have been printed the sheets of paper will be folded in a special way, which will make all the pages the right side up again.

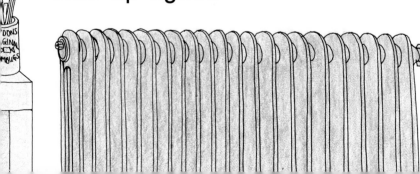

The very large sheets with pages on them are then photographed by a big camera. It makes a piece of film for each separate color.

This is done by putting color filters in front of the lens to take out all the other colors.

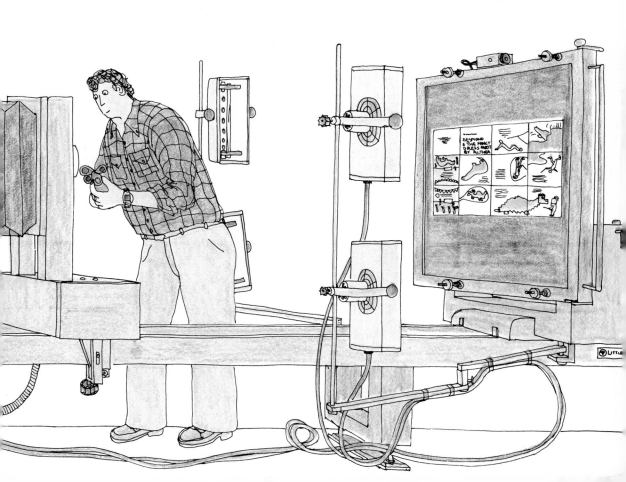

The book will be printed in dots of four colors: red, blue, yellow and black. Other colors are made by printing these four colors on top of each other. For instance, if you print blue on top of yellow it makes green.

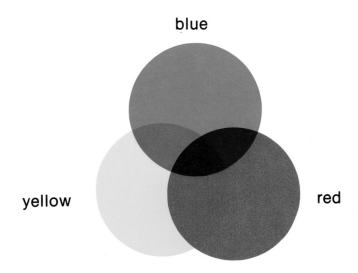

The film is developed in an automatic processor.

The developed film is then put in the enlarger to make a second film.

The new film can be made bigger
or smaller than the original artwork.
A fine screen is put in front of the new film
to break the picture up into dots.

If you look at a picture through a magnifying
glass you can see the dots of color.

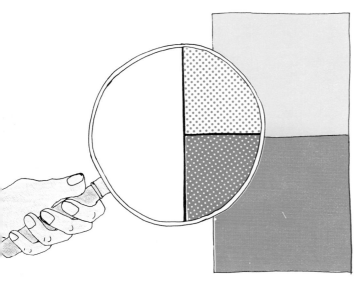

A light patch of color
lets less light
through the screen and
so exposes the small
dots on the film.

A strong patch of color
lets bright spots of light
through the screen
which exposes big dots
on the film.

Using powerful lights which shine through the film, the image on the film is then transferred on to a thin metal sheet. This is called a printing plate.

The platemaker rubs the plate with special developing liquid, and slowly the pictures and words appear on it.

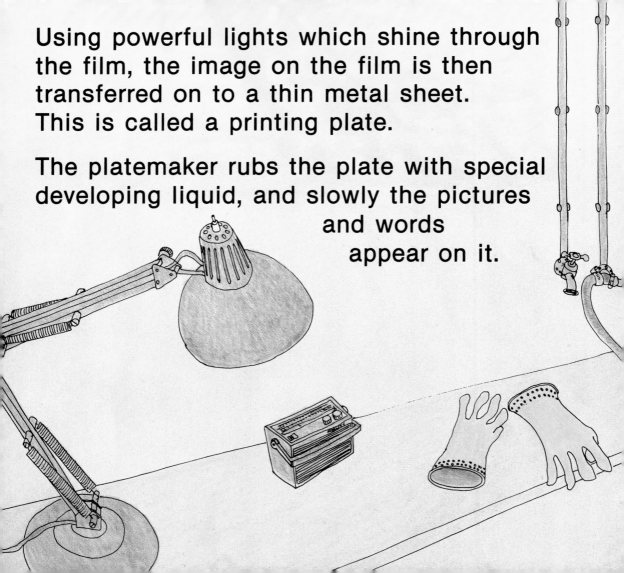

Here is the
printing plate.

The printing plate is bent around a big cylinder on the printing press. The book is being printed on a press which can print two colors at a time, so a plate is attached to each of its two cylinders. The first two inks are put into the ink trays.

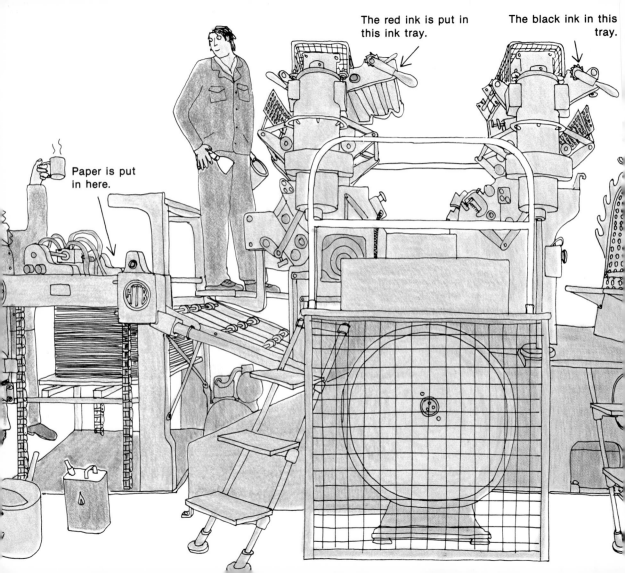

The red ink is put in this ink tray.

The black ink in this tray.

Paper is put in here.

Printed sheets.

The sheet of paper is to be printed in four colors on each side.
So, after printing with the blue and yellow they will change the plates and clean the press. Then they will print red and black.

The paper will have to go through the printing press twice on each side.

The covers are printed in the same way, but on much thicker paper. Sometimes they are put through another press which rolls varnish all over them to make them shiny. When this is done it is very sticky, so the cover must be allowed to dry for several hours.

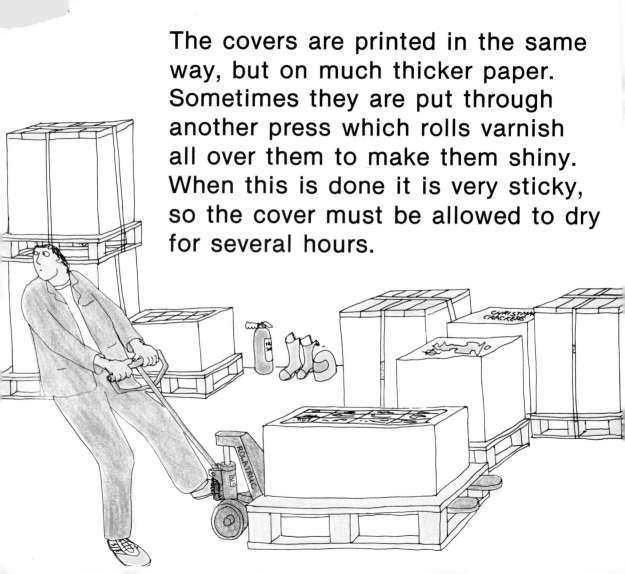

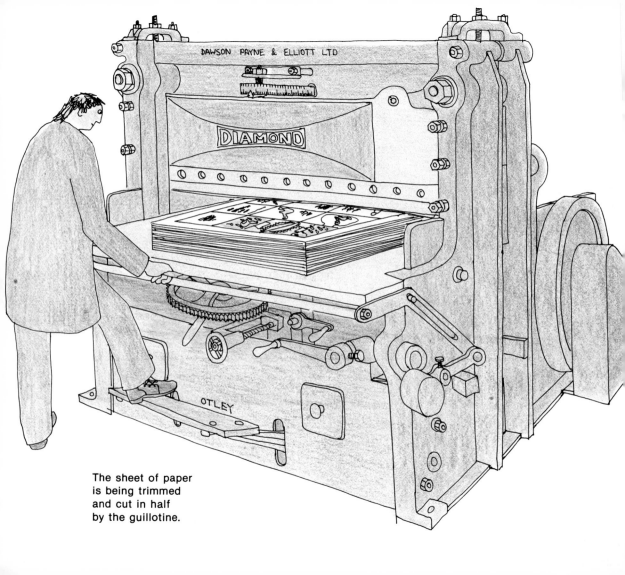

The sheet of paper
is being trimmed
and cut in half
by the guillotine.

The sheets of paper now have all the pages
of the book printed on them. They are
trimmed and cut in half, then put through
a machine which folds each half into
twelve pages.

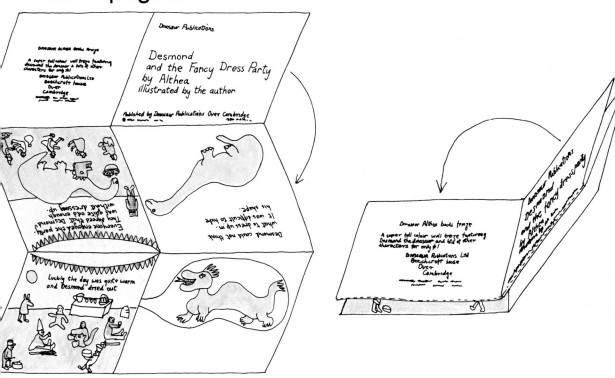

The two halves of the book and the cover are dropped on to each other. The book is stitched through the middle with two pieces of wire, which are bent like staples.

First half of the book drops down on the conveyor.

The second half of the book drops on top.

Now the cover is folded and dropped on the pages.

The stitcher is putting in the wire stitches.
↓

The machine closes the book and trims it on three of its sides to cut away the folds. Now it can be opened and read. This is how to make a paperback book.

The book is being closed.

Three knife trimmers cut away the folds.

Finished books.